Saying Goodbye To Nanny

Lorna Vyse

Illustrated by Jenn Garside

Copyright © 2024 Lorna Vyse

ISBN: 978-1-7396594-4-8

The right of Lorna Vyse to be identified as the author of this work has been asserted by her in accordance with the Copyright, Designs and Patents Act 1988.

All rights reserved. No part of this book may be reproduced, stored in a retrieval system, or transmitted in any form or by any means, including electronic, mechanical, photocopying, recording or otherwise, without the prior written permission of the copyright holder, except in the case of brief quotations in printed reviews.

This is a work of fiction. Names, titles, characters, businesses, places, events, and incidents are either the products of the author's imagination or used in a fictitious manner. Any resemblance to actual persons, living or dead, or actual events is purely coincidental.

A CIP record of this book is available from the British Library.

Printed in the UK.

Illustrated by Jenn Garside

For my nannies, both named Ivy
– with love x

Children call their grandparents by lots of different names. Most grandmothers decide what they want to be called and here are some names they can choose from:

Gran   nana   Nan
Granny   Grandma
gan gan   Grammy
Nanny   Nanna

My name is Ivy-Rose.

This story is about one of my grandparents – my Nanny. She was a very special lady in my life.

Let me introduce you to Nanny and Grandad, my Daddy's parents.

Their real names are Pat and Mike, but I know them as Nanny Flowers (as she loved pretty flowers) and Grandad Birds (as he feeds the birds in his garden every day).

I loved being with them both.

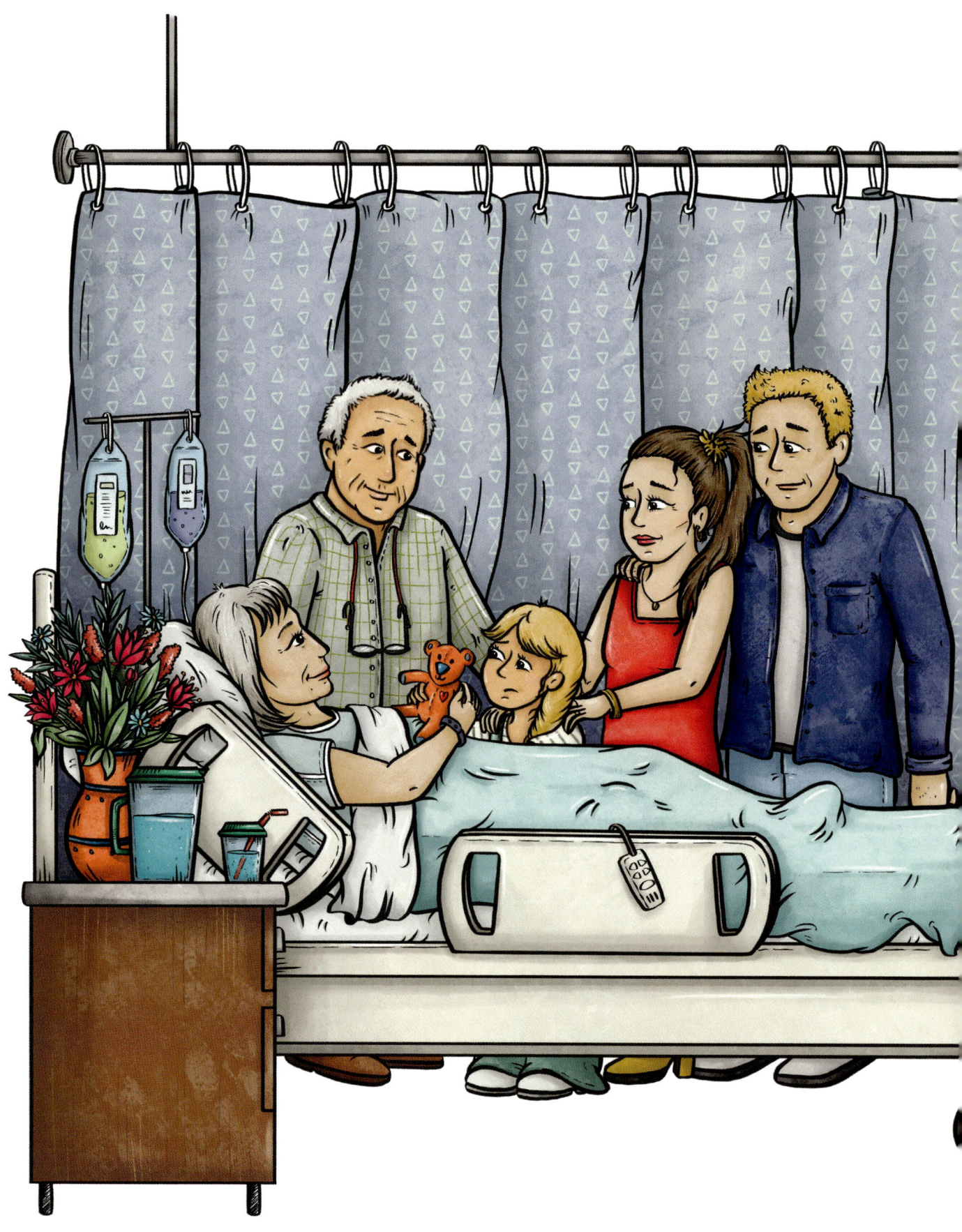

With her silky grey hair, big smile and squeaky laugh, Nanny often made me giggle. We spent lots of time together, playing games and making fairy cakes (my favourite). But then she started feeling ill, so we couldn't see each other as often.

Nanny went to the doctors to see if they could help her feel better. They sent her in an ambulance to hospital so she could rest and recover. Mummy said the doctors needed to do some tests to find out what was wrong with her and to give her some medicine.

The doctors said that Nanny had to stay in hospital for a few days, so we went to see her. I took one of my teddies to keep her company in case she was feeling lonely. We went to the ward she was on and I found myself staring at Nanny a lot. She looked a bit different somehow. We chatted about my day at school and I told her that I had got 9 out of 12 in my spelling test. She said I was very clever, which made me smile as I had been feeling a bit upset that I got three words wrong.

Nanny kept putting her head on her pillow and shutting her eyes. I thought she must be very tired. I was worried about her because I hadn't seen her like that before. I wondered how long it would be before the medicines worked. It felt too scary to ask any of the adults in the room.

A few days later, Mummy told me that she and Daddy had been to the hospital to see Nanny while I was at school. We all sat together and Mummy snuggled me close. She spoke quietly as she said that Nanny was very, very ill, and the doctors had tried everything they could to make her better, but nothing was working.

Daddy explained that Nanny's body had stopped working properly and the medicines weren't going to be able to help. With tears in his eyes, he told me that Nanny was going to die.

I started crying. I felt so upset and confused. I didn't want it to be true. I had been so sure that she was going to get better and I'd been looking forward to her coming home.

My world had turned upside down and I had no idea what would happen now.

I had so many questions going around in my head so I decided to speak to Mummy.

When will Nanny die?

It's hard to know exactly when someone will die when they are seriously ill. It depends on so many things as our bodies stop working properly and start to shut down completely. Our breathing slows right down and then our heart stops and our life ends.

Nanny is coming to the end of her life but she is being well looked after by the doctors and nurses. They will make sure that she's feeling comfortable and isn't in pain.

Can I visit Nanny again before she dies?

Nanny is allowed to have visitors so you, Daddy and I will go and see her together. Grandad will be there too. We won't be able to stay very long, though. Nanny is feeling very tired and she sleeps quite a lot now. That's because her body is starting to slow down.

We can spend some precious time with her and tell her how much we all love her.

Perhaps you can draw her a picture or write her a letter? I know she would really like that. We will each be able to say our own special goodbye to her, which is important as she is now coming to the end of her life and our time together. It is very sad for all of us.

Later, I sat in my bedroom and thought about Nanny and what she liked doing most and what would make her smile. She loved sitting in her garden so I drew her a bright, colourful picture of a garden full of pretty flowers.

The next day, we all went to visit Nanny at a place called a hospice.

It was a bit different to the hospital – to me it felt smaller and much brighter. Mummy explained that a hospice is a place where people who are seriously ill can go to be looked after in the days and weeks before they die. I was worried about going to the hospice because I thought it would be sad and scary, but I quite liked it. Everyone was very kind and friendly.

A lady who worked at the hospice asked if I wanted to choose a fabric heart to give to Nanny. She explained that if Nanny and I each had one of the hearts then we would always be connected. I chose a pack of two small hearts that were decorated with pretty purple spots.

Nanny had her own bedroom with yellow walls and lots of colourful pictures. Her room had two wide doors that led out to a small garden that was full of plants and flowers and surrounded by some tall trees. Stepping outside, I saw lots of different birds flying around, landing on the neat green grass and eating seeds from a bird feeder. *They will make Nanny very happy*, I thought.

I wasn't worried any more.

Next to Nanny's bed was a photo of her, Grandad and all our family. I knew Nanny would like that, too.

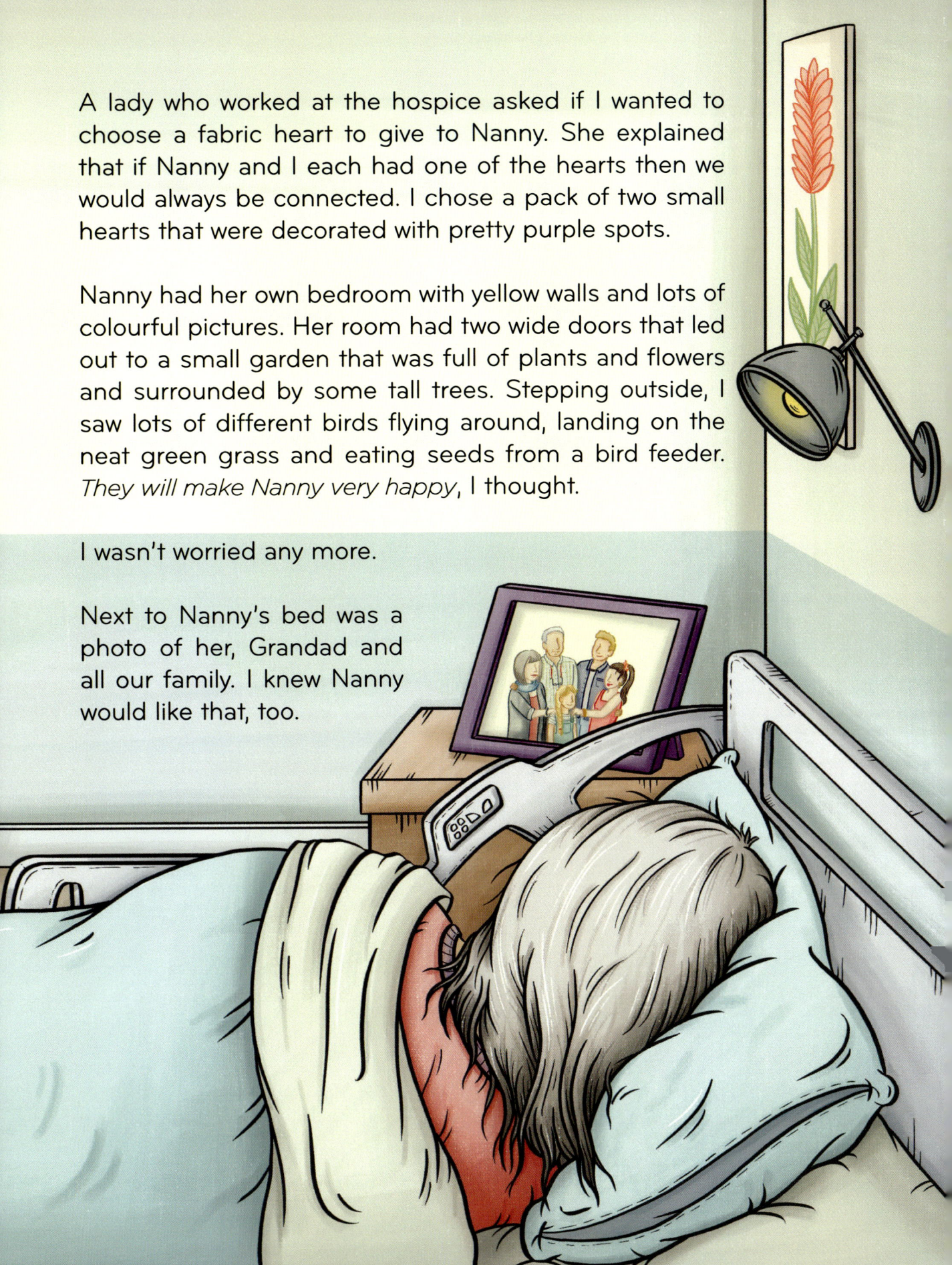

I spoke softly to Nanny when she opened her eyes. "I love you loads and I've missed you", I said. She squeezed my hand and said she'd missed me too. I noticed a tear run down her cheek when I proudly presented her with my picture and the spotty fabric heart. I held onto mine tightly.

"I have a heart, too", I told her. "They're both exactly the same!"

I liked the little poem on the card that came with them, so I read it out to Nanny.

> "These little hearts connect us two.
> I will hold mine close and think of you.
> Keep the other safe and think of me.
> Then together linked we will always be."

Then it was time to leave and for me to say my special goodbye. I cuddled Nanny and said, "Goodbye, Nanny. I love you." She hugged me back and whispered, "Goodbye, Sweet Pea. I love you very much and always will."

When I got home from school a couple of days later, Daddy told me in a very soft voice that Nanny had died. I burst into tears. Mummy and Daddy had been crying too. I could tell. We were all very sad.

I suddenly felt scared. It was frightening to think that I wouldn't ever see Nanny again. I spent some time just sitting and staring into space while stroking our family dog, Henry. He was always willing to sit with me and snuggle and his fur was soft to touch. It was comforting. Henry seemed to know that everyone in the family was feeling sad and that we all needed extra doggy cuddles.

I realised that I wasn't exactly sure what being dead meant. Well, not completely sure. How could we be certain that Nanny had died?

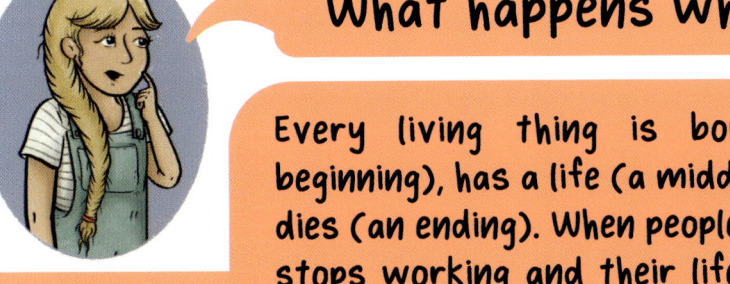

What happens when people die?

Every living thing is born (it has a beginning), has a life (a middle bit) and then dies (an ending). When people die, their body stops working and their life comes to an end. It is not like being asleep. Their heart stops beating, and they stop breathing. When you die you can't see, hear, think, speak or feel anything.

It can often be very hard for us when people die as we can miss them so much.

Over the next few days, Grandad and Daddy planned Nanny's funeral, which they said was going to be a celebration of her life. They talked about lots of different things, like burial and cremation, some of which I didn't understand.

Daddy said that funerals are a way of saying goodbye to people who have died. Their family and friends come together at a special service to remember them and talk about the things they did in their life.

I wanted to remember Nanny. I wanted to talk to family and friends about the things she did during her life. I asked if I could go to her funeral. Mummy and Daddy said yes.

What is a burial and what's cremation?

When someone dies, their body is placed in a coffin, which is a special type of box. If they are going to be buried, the coffin is put deep into the ground in a hole called a grave. When someone is cremated, the coffin is put into a very hot burner (called a cremator) that turns the body and the coffin into ashes.

People don't like to think about this too much, but it's important to remember that a burial or cremation won't hurt the person who has died. They can't see, hear, feel, touch or breathe any more.

Families can usually choose whether their loved ones have a burial or a cremation, and sometimes people have shared their wishes with those they feel closest to before they die. This can be helpful for families as they know exactly what the person wants.

Just like Mummy said, Nanny's body was put into a coffin. The little fabric heart that I gave her at the hospice was put in the coffin with her, together with a letter and picture from me, and some purple flowers I had chosen to go on top. I was pleased about all of that. The coffin was taken to the funeral in a big black car, called a hearse.

Songs were played during the service and Grandad spoke about Nanny and her kindness to everyone. Lots of people were crying. I cried too, but Mummy told me that was okay. I held my little fabric heart tightly in my hand.

We would all miss Nanny.

After the funeral service, Nanny's coffin was taken to a cemetery near to where we lived and put in the grave. It felt a bit weird watching the box going down into the ground, but I couldn't look away. I knew that the earth would be put back in place when we went home, and a little plaque with Nanny's name would be put there so we would know that was where she was buried. Grandad had told me.

The day after the funeral, I went back to school. I kept getting upset when I thought about Nanny and her funeral. I felt sad. I missed her so much.

Mummy had already told my teachers that Nanny had died, so the adults in school were extra kind to me. Before I stepped into my classroom that morning, my teacher explained that she had already told the class my news, so everyone knew why I hadn't been in school. That's what Mummy and I had agreed before I went back.

At break time, some friends asked me what had happened, so I told them about Nanny, her illness and her funeral. As I told them my story, it almost felt like it had happened to someone else, not my family. My friends hugged me, held my hand and asked me to play games with them and that helped me feel much better.

My best friend Liam said he would look after me. He was so kind and caring and he helped me a lot. He told the teacher when I was upset. A member of the school team had a chat with me, on my own, and we talked about Nanny and how I was feeling. I liked talking to them about Nanny. It made me feel like she hadn't been forgotten.

One weekend, not long after Nanny's funeral, Mummy said she thought we should make a memory box together. We chose a box and talked about Nanny while we put things inside. We found a necklace she had really liked, a bottle of her perfume and some photos of us with Nanny. We also put my little fabric heart in. The heart was so special to me, even more so since Nanny had died. Whenever I held it, I knew Nanny and I were connected in some way, just like the poem said.

I knew I could look at the box whenever I wanted to remember how important Nanny was to me. We chatted and agreed that it might be good to look at the box at special times, like Christmas and Nanny's birthday in September.

I tucked the box with all its treasures safely away under my bed.

I showed it to Grandad when he came to visit us. He liked it too and promised to find a few more things of Nanny's that could be put in my box. That made me feel so happy and I was excited to see what Grandad would choose for me.

Some days I felt sad or angry and sometimes I was confused. I didn't really understand why Nanny had to get ill and leave us. I missed her so much.

I got very cross with Mummy one day when we were baking. She wasn't making the cakes in the right way – not like Nanny made them. I stamped my feet and shouted, "No Mummy, not like that!" She stared at me, looking shocked. I put my hands on my hips and demanded to see Nanny right now, as she knew how to do things properly.

But Nanny had died, so she couldn't come back and help me with baking or anything else. For a moment I had forgotten. But then I remembered.

Mummy's arms pulled me towards her, holding me close as I burst into tears. Mummy cried, too.

Some things would take time to get used to.

Walking in from school one day, I saw Grandad sitting at our kitchen table. In front of him was a large clear jar with a bright blue lid. Next to it was a rainbow of felt tip pens and strips of brightly coloured paper. I wondered if Grandad had brought us a new biscuit jar, but that seemed odd.

Grandad smiled. "We're going to make a memory jar together", he said. "Mummy and Daddy are doing it with us, too. Choose a piece of paper and write a memory or thought about Nanny on it." We all sat at the table and wrote memories of Nanny. We read them out to each other before popping them in the jar. Some of our memories made us laugh and some made us sad, but it was so nice to share them all.

We wrote a label that said 'Memories of Nanny Jar' and stuck it to the front of the jar. Then we put it on the bookcase so we could add more notes whenever we wanted to and look at it any time (on our own or as a family).

Where do people go when they die?

Nobody really knows for sure what happens after a person's physical body is buried or cremated. This means that we can all have our own beliefs and thoughts, and no one can tell us that they are wrong.

Some people's beliefs are based on their culture or religion, while other people just believe in what feels comforting. Some people believe in Heaven and being reunited with their God and others believe in reincarnation, where the person goes on to be born again in a different life. Other people believe that when you die, that is simply the end.

People can believe that a dead person's spirit or soul returns to life in a different form. Some people believe birds (for example, robins), insects (like dragonflies) or animals could be their loved ones returning to visit them. Many feel they can talk to the person after they have died. All of these beliefs can help people feel close to their loved one and give them comfort that they might be nearby.

I like to think that Nanny is in a good place and she is happy wherever she is. I feel she is near to us in some way, although we can't see or hear her. I like to think that she will always be in our hearts, and that means she's never far away. You can take your time to decide what you would like to believe.

Today was Nanny's birthday. Normally, this was a special day in the year to celebrate as a family, but this year it was different.

We all visited the cemetery and took Nanny some beautiful pink and purple flowers to place on her grave. Where the small plaque had once been there was now a gravestone. It told the world who she was and that she was a wife, a mum and my nanny. I liked that.

Even though it was Nanny's birthday, Grandad gave me a present. He knew Nanny used to love buying gifts for people, so he thought it would be a nice idea. I thought it was a great plan because I liked getting presents! He gave me a photograph of Nanny holding me as a baby. She was wearing a lovely flowery top and a purple jumper. He said the tops were some of her favourites, so he had asked someone to make them into a memory bear for me. It was such a special bear – not a toy – made especially for me. I loved it. I carefully put it in my bedroom so I could see it every day.

We all sat down together to read the notes we had put in our 'Memories of Nanny Jar' over the past few months. We all cried at times as we looked through them, but we also laughed a lot as we remembered all the funny and kind things Nanny had done for us.

Grandad said that looking at all those notes on Nanny's birthday had helped him feel a bit better because we were all talking about her. He wanted to make it a new family tradition and we all agreed with him. We even added some more notes that day with little messages of love to Nanny.

So much has changed since Nanny died. It has been hard, but some things really helped me to understand what was happening and gave me ways to remember her. I know other children in my class have had a much-loved grandparent die, too, so I wrote a list of things that might help them and other children and I'm sharing it for everyone to see.

It can be a sad and lonely time when someone close to you dies. You often feel you are the only one going through it, so I hope my tips and ideas help someone out there.

I know I will never forget my Nanny. She was so special.

Wherever she is, I know that she still loves me and that I love her. We will always be connected.

Ivy-Rose's 'Top 10 Tips' to help you if someone important in your life is seriously ill or has died

1. Lots of things can change when someone you know is seriously ill or has died – but you will be okay.

2. You might feel sad, angry, confused, guilty or worried, but that's all normal.

3. It's okay to cry if you're upset. Don't feel you have to hide your tears.

4. Most adults will want to try to help and support you, but sometimes you need to give them some ideas about what is best for you.

5. Write down or draw things to help you understand what is happening and how you are feeling.

6. Remember that it's always okay to talk about the person who is ill or has died.

7. Ask for a 'time-out card' at school. It means you can leave class if you ever get upset, and the adults in school will know you need some extra support.

8. If you have a pet, spend time with them. You can tell them anything and they won't tell anyone else!

9. Make a memory box so you will always remember your important person.

10. Always ask questions if there is anything you are unsure of or don't understand about what's happening. You can never ask a silly question.

Acknowledgements

Thank you to everyone who has encouraged me to write this book to support children who have experienced the death of a beloved grandparent. I hope that my efforts make a difference to children as they come to terms with their grief.

My heartfelt thanks go to all the children and young people who have shared their stories with me over the years; stories of those they have loved who have died. It has been a privilege.

Special thanks go to a few people who have given me their time and support once again, namely Sophie, Andrea, Ali, Cyan, Lisa and also Nicola at Norfolk Hospice. You have all believed in my ability to be a children's author and I thank you for that and for your views and guidance throughout my journey. Thank you to Jenn Garside for your ongoing care and attention with the illustrations and layout and Maddy Edwards for your editing skills.

A final, heartfelt thanks to my husband Steve and my family – for bringing me cups of tea and giving general reassurance when I've had numerous ideas swirling in my head. I will be eternally grateful.

About the Author

Lorna Vyse is a qualified Child Bereavement Specialist passionate about supporting children and young people who have experienced the death of someone important in their lives. She has nearly three decades of experience working with children of all ages in a variety of youth and community settings, mostly in the voluntary sector.

Lorna has supported numerous children, young people and their families during their bereavement journey. She recognises the challenges faced and the emotional impact that grief can have on young lives. She is determined to improve access to information and guidance for children about dying, death and bereavement. She seeks opportunities to champion the needs of bereaved children and ensure that their voices are heard.

Lorna has already written a collection of three children's bereavement support books, as well as many accompanying resources. Details can be found on her website.

Website: www.lornavyse.com

Other books by the Author

Ellie's Book: The Story of When My Mummy Died
ISBN: 978-1-7396594-0-0

Ben's Book: The Story of When My Mum Died
ISBN: 978-1-7396594-1-7

Alex's Book: The Story of When My Mum Died
ISBN: 978-1-7396594-2-4